Praise for *Adult Human Male*

Transness queers *everything*, which is why so many people are so
frightened by it. Oliver Radclyffe has described his own growth and
change, and how it felt from the inside. In doing, so he has predicted
a future in which gender is not just mutable, but trivial. I can't wait to
live in that world, and I love Oliver for forging the path.

Janet W. Hardy

Oliver Radclyffe's *Adult Human Male* is an excoriating response
to what he calls the "hostile cis perspective" — the lie that there are
no trans people, just broken cisgender people … But it is more:
Interweaving his own story with the political, he makes the fight
personal by letting us know him. After *Adult Human Male,* we cannot
be neutral — anyone reading it can say they know a trans man and can
put a face to the headlines. He writes with deft prose and measured
fury, centering himself, his body, as the real thing being attacked in
this fight … In Radclyffe's hands, transness becomes intimate and
undeniably real.

Alexander Cheves

In *Adult Human Male,* Oliver Radclyffe answers any question you
could ever think of to explain what it feels like to be trans in every
sense — bodily, politically, socially — and then some, giving us insight
into a future where gender is more flexible than two categories … He
does so plainly, with a dry humor and a gentle but firm hand that
refuses to cede an inch of ground when it comes to the sovereignty of
trans bodies and trans lives … His monograph is a moment of literary
calm amid the wild seas of our current political and cultural landscape.

Sophia Anfinn Tonnessen

Adult
Human Male

Adult
Human Male Oliver
Radclyffe

UNBOUND EDITION PRESS

Atlanta

FIRST EDITION

Printed in the United States of America

LIBRARY OF CONGRESS RECORD

Name: Radclyffe, Oliver, 1971 — author.
Title: Adult Human Male / Oliver Radclyffe.
Edition: First edition.
Published: Atlanta : Unbound Edition Press, 2023.

LCCN: 2023935036
LCCN Permalink: https://lccn.loc.gov/2023935036
ISBN: 979-8-9870199-7-9 (fine softcover)

Designed by Eleanor Safe and Joseph Floresca
Printed by Bookmobile, Minneapolis, MN
Distributed by Itasca Books

123456789

Unbound Edition Press
1270 Caroline Street, Suite D120
Box 448
Atlanta, GA 30307

*The Unbound Edition Press logo and name are
registered trademarks of Unbound Edition LLC.*

For my Mum and Dad

Thank you for listening.

Contents

1. Perspective   15

2. Body   25

3. Fences   39

4. Procreation   51

5. Second Act   59

6. The Future   67

Adult
Human Male

The sound of trumpets died away
and Orlando stood stark naked. No
human being, since the world began,
has ever looked more ravishing.

Virginia Woolf

1. Perspective

My mother is an epistolary activist. She writes letters from her head-quarters, which are set up at the kitchen table of an old farmhouse buried deep in the English countryside. So far, the recipients of her letters have included the Archbishop of Canterbury, the Prime Minister, Sir Ian McKellen, and occasionally — by proxy — my father.

"I wish to express my very deep concern that you have not yet acknowledged that a court order should not be necessary for a young person in need of clinically recommended gender-affirming treat-ment," she writes to the head of the National Health Service. "I would have thought that the requirement may very well be illegal, considering the High Court ruling that parents are able to give consent on their child's behalf. I hope that you will address this issue immediately, since it seems to me that you are deliberately disobeying the law of the land, and as a highly respected organization you have a duty of care toward marginalized members of the public."

Don't mess with my mother. She may be a septuagenarian with arthritis and a hearing-aid, but she knows how to write a letter.

One day she sent me an email asking for my help. She and my father had got into a bit of a tiff over an opinion piece in *The Times* (of London) condemning the use of hormone blockers, and she wanted to pen a letter to the editor to state her position on the matter. Her plan was to show this letter to my father before sending it.

"I'd like to prepare a simple, straightforward response so that the readers (and your father) can understand the objective facts," she said. "Do you think you might find an article that explains the issue in a balanced way?" When I suggested I draft her a response myself, my offer was politely rebuffed. "Your father thinks you're too invested in the issue to be objective. What he wants is a neutral, unbiased opinion. Perhaps something written by someone he trusts?"

What my mother was asking for was an opinion held by an educated, white, heterosexual man, preferably an established journalist from one of the mainstream, if right-wing, newspapers. My father didn't want a neutral opinion; he wanted an opinion written from his perspective, and my mother was trying to provide it for him.

Even before I started looking, I knew it was a fool's mission, because it's almost impossible to find an article written by someone my father respects who is willing to take the needs of trans people into consideration. The problem isn't that all cis white male journalists are transphobic, it's just that their reporting tends to skew toward the needs of cis people. They're unaware of the degree to which their own identities influence not only which part of our lives they focus on, but also the language they use and the angle they take.

The cis perspective might seem universal, but it's by no means neutral. It's a specific point of view with its own set of cognitive biases and cultural privileges. The trans perspective isn't neutral either, but the cis perspective currently holds all the power. This isn't just due to the gross imbalance in numbers between cis and trans people; it's also because the society in which we live was created by people who believed in the gender binary, and this belief system is now so deeply embedded into our culture and language that most people barely notice it's there.

When most of the information available to cis people about trans issues is being supplied by cis journalists, from a cis perspective, using cis-centric language, the needs of trans people usually disappear from the conversation.

And that's the best-case scenario. A journalist who is taking an actively transphobic stance won't just ignore our needs, they'll pick them up and use them against us. We are disfiguring our bodies, or indulging our mental illnesses, or perverting the course of nature — or so they will say. And if the audience is listening to a debate in which one side is confirming their worldview and the other side destabilizes it, it's not hard to guess in whose direction they'll lean. So, these transphobic journalists are emboldened to continue to use culturally familiar language to draw pictures of trans people as dangerous or disturbed over and over again — burning these toxic images into people's minds — while we remain trapped in the corner in crouch position.

> *We can disagree and still love each other, unless your*
> *disagreement is rooted in my oppression and denial of*
> *my humanity and right to exist.*

James Baldwin

"Why can't we have a reasonable, balanced debate?" is something I hear quite regularly. If it's a friend asking, this question is usually followed by a wistful sigh that not everyone is as "easy to talk to" as I am. If it's someone in the press or on social media, it's usually followed by mentions of angry mobs, gender cults, pronoun police, and women being silenced.

"I'd love a reasonable, balanced debate," I reply. Truly, I would.

Pleasant amicability is my default setting. I was raised in England, so politeness is my first language. I have four children, so I know how to stay cool during reactive conversations. And I've had enough relationships to know that clear, calm communication is my love language. I should be able to engage in a reasonable, balanced debate.

And yet I can't, because the debate is about my body, and you can't stand in ideological opposition to a body. You can object to it, or try to control it, or demand governance over it, but that's not a point of view. That's authoritarianism.

My mother sent me the opinion piece from *The Times* that had caused her marital friction. I'm familiar with the journalist; she's one of many writers out there claiming to write our unauthorized biographies.

The writers are professors and academics, journalists and economists, psychiatrists and sexologists, all of them experts in their fields. The books and articles they write are carefully constructed and meticulously researched, based on empirical evidence, accumulated data, and scientifically irrefutable facts. And yet, as far as I can tell, they are all getting the same fundamental thing wrong.

These writers are not writing about trans people. One of them even admits as much in the introduction to their book. Instead, they tell terrifying stories of cis people who've been duped into believing they're trans, or cis people trying to convince everyone that they're trans, or cis people in the grip of some strange paraphilia, or cis people who are mentally ill. There are no trans people in these books, because according to their authors, nobody is trans.

Such books engage in stochastic terrorism. They are purposeful. They demonize and dehumanize; they speak in terms of implicit danger and moral degeneration. They claim to wish no harm on the people who continue — against good advice — to identify as trans-gender, and yet their insistence that we pose a threat to women and children tacitly encourages aggression against us, not just in the form of anti-trans legislation, but also in the form of physical violence. And if you go to great lengths to warn people of an imminent threat, you must take some responsibility when some of those people decide to rise up in arms against it.

The trans conversation has become a pinball machine and we are the ball; sometimes we're pinged around so fast it's hard to tell who the enemy is.

Terrifying evangelical pastors running for Republican office who call trans people a national security threat and then appeal for the reinstatement of a McCarthy-era committee so that we can be tried and executed for treason are clearly transphobic. Nice, polite, white ladies asking that we continue to protect the rights of women and children are harder to call out. But the people in the back room who make the ammunition are equally as dangerous as the people out front who shoot the guns.

But look, the books are useful: at least they show us the lens through which we are being seen. I don't like being written about without my permission, and I don't much like being viewed through that particular lens. But, then again, I've just finished writing another book in which I write quite a bit about other people (seen through my lens, without their permission) so I probably don't have a leg to stand on. The difference is that I'm not trying to erase an entire community.

On some level I understand where the fear is coming from; we appear to have surfaced out of nowhere, and to receive the legal protections and medical care we need, we have had to make a lot of noise. It's true that our stories often focus on murder, suicide and hate crimes, and this may sound hyperbolic to some. We wish it weren't so; we shouldn't have to use avoiding death as the reason for allowing us to transition, but this is the corner we've been backed into. We have had to tell everyone how terrible dysphoria feels in order to explain why access to gender affirming care is so necessary, but this has the undesired side-effect of making them want to prevent this terrible experience from happening to anyone they love, which has resulted in what I refer to as the hostile cis perspective. And every time we speak, we provide more fuel for their fire, but if we turn down the noise nothing will change.

To be clear, by "hostile" I don't mean angry or aggressive; I mean innately hostile to the idea of transition. The hostile cis perspective assumes that everyone is cisgender, and therefore opposes any attempt — either social or medical — to interfere with this supposed norm. Are they transphobic? They wouldn't use that term. The whole concept of transphobia is immaterial if nobody is trans. The primary purpose of the hostile cis perspective is to preserve cisgenderism at all costs; to protect cis people from the horrors of accidental trans-identification or transition. That is all that matters.

The problem is that the only way for these people to continue in their belief that we don't exist is by disregarding almost everything we have to say, because nothing we say about ourselves aligns with anything they say about us, and they must be right, or they'd have to stop talking. They try very hard not to hear us, and when this fails, they focus their energy on coming up with clever ways to discredit our perspective. Presumably they're hoping that if they center themselves hard enough, eventually we might just fall off the edge of the conversation.

It might seem surprising that people who are not trans should be trying so vehemently to center their voices in the conversation about being trans, but viewed from the hostile cis perspective it makes perfect sense. If you truly believe that trans people are actually dangerous or delusional cis people, then you become the voice of a distorted reason. You're on a crusade to defend humanity. Of course, your voice should be central. After all, it always has been.

But an argument for the legal erasure of trans care is an argument for forced assimilation. And forced assimilation has historically been a rather bloody ordeal.

So, if you do believe that trans people exist, then the desire of this vocal opposition to remove all the necessary resources for the entire trans community starts to look a little different. Like, frighteningly different. Like, maybe genocide? It all depends on your perspective.

It's more than a little scary over here on the edge.

✚ ✚ ✚

Once you become aware of the hostile cis perspective, you see it everywhere. The problem is that other people often don't, so when you flag it, you're accused of hyper-sensitivity, of trying to silence the opposition, or aggressively obstructing a so-called "both-sides" debate.

Not everyone who enters this debate is trying to eliminate us, obviously, but even journalists who claim to be allies of the trans community can end up doing harm if they prioritize the needs of cis people at the expense of the needs of trans people. In a fair and equal society, it might not be such a problem, but right now the intensity of the attacks against us have turned what might otherwise be healthy, open conversation into a zero-sum game. It can never be an equal conversation when one side is attacking so hard that all the other side can do is defend. We don't want to be stuck here at trans 101 — continually justifying our right to exist — but until the bloodhounds are called off, we're going to be too busy trying to protect ourselves to elevate the conversation to the next level.

One of the obvious solutions is to make room for more trans people to write about trans issues: Employ more trans journalists in the mainstream media, persuade the television newscasters, commentators and hosts to platform more trans people, and allow us to speak. But before this can happen, the cis writers and speakers who currently fill those positions would have to acknowledge that however experienced they may be, however many years they've been reporting, however many awards they've won, they only have a limited ability to tell our stories. And nobody likes to have their abilities questioned. Nobody likes being asked to cede authority, particularly to a trans person.

The cis perspective is not neutral. This bears repeating. And my transness is not ideological. An assault on my right to be trans is an assault on my life.

I remember who my mother was before she met me. She truly believed in the goodness of humanity, the decency of ordinary people. And I understood her impulse to shy away from using the word transphobic; she found it hard to accept that there were people out there who really wanted us gone. Surely their intentions were honorable, even if their methods were suspect?

It makes me sad that my mother is no longer the sweet, young innocent she used to be, but that's what happens when your parents finally grow up.

So, my mother continues her letter-writing crusade. She writes to the people who might be persuaded by the anti-trans rhetoric in the newspapers, decent people who (she is certain) really want to do the right thing, but who don't have all the necessary information. She still believes in the power of persuasion; she writes in good faith.

My admiration for my mother — and her conviction that she can change the world one middle-class white person at a time — will never waver. But sometimes when I read her letters, I wonder to whom she's really writing. Perhaps she's writing to her friends, who she's afraid to speak with in case they tell her how they really feel. Perhaps she's writing to my father, trying to make sure we all stay on the same page.

Or perhaps she's writing to herself, to the person she was before I transitioned: the woman who also once believed all the things she read in the newspapers.

Adult Human Male

2. Body

When Orlando fell asleep after a party in Constantinople and woke up with a different body, Virginia Woolf tried not to make a big deal out of it. She transitioned her protagonist through male, nonbinary, and female pronouns in the space of a few sentences, deftly sidestepped the question of how or why it had happened by feigning boredom, and then moved on with her story. She assumed, as loyal readers, that we would accept her version of events — that Orlando was now a woman — and so we did.

Woolf had full creative license over Orlando's body, just as I have over mine. Texts have bodies. Bodies have stories. I am the author of mine, both.

I have accumulated maleness and become the sum of my parts. The inventory of my parts are as follows:

One hairline, receding; one pair of eyebrows, un-plucked; one jawline, stubbled; one Adam's apple; one back, muscled; one chest, scarred; two forearms, tattooed; two hands, veined; one stomach, flat(ish); one penis, not visible; one pair of hips, narrow; two legs, hairy; one pair of feet.

Imagine you walk into a coffee shop one morning and you see someone sitting at a table. They're wearing jeans, boots and a shirt with the sleeves rolled up to their elbows, they're reading a newspaper and drinking a cup of coffee. Your brain does a swift calculation. It adds up the sum of their parts (listed above) and draws a conclusion: man drinking coffee. Do you accept the evidence of your own eyes? Or are the hidden assets — the chromosomes, reproductive organs and genitalia — more important to you? When someone tells you they are a man or a woman, do you believe them? If not, how far are you willing to go to prove they are not who they say they are? And how do you choose from which parts of their body you select the evidence to back up your claim?

Once upon a time, when you entered that coffee shop, your eyes would have told you that I was a woman.

Does this mean that I was a woman before and I'm a man now, or that I was always a man, or that I'm still a woman?

I was born into a body that, given the fact that I am a man, developed incorrectly in the womb and continued to develop incorrectly throughout puberty. There are medical solutions for this now, but to believe you can correct a physical error, first you have to believe it is one. You must enter the trans reality.

I'll let you into mine if you make room for me in yours.

✢ ✢ ✢

The hair on my lower belly appeared first, forming a little blond shaft that curled upwards. Soon after, I started finding little balls of fluff secreted inside my bellybutton. My new stomach hairs weren't passive or inert; they'd been gathering dust, knitting it into little balls and depositing it into the receptacle provided. It felt both delicate and intentional, like my body had found a new hobby.

My great-aunt invented a word for bellybutton fluff — or the unidentifiable lint lodged behind the sofa cushions, or the felted pellets of dust and dog hair that collect under the fridge — *mushquoise*. It was a made-up word, but it sounded exactly right, and it served a good purpose. I didn't realize it wasn't in the dictionary until I was an adult. But my great-aunt wasn't trying to pervert language, she just wanted to create a new word where she believed a word needed to exist.

The dictionary says gender is a "division" or a "category" of human beings. The only thing this tells us is that we invented a word to separate people.

We demand much too much from gender. Nobody could possibly live up to the kind of expectations we place on this one little word. We use it to refer to roles (which are socially constructed) and expression (which is a personal choice) and identity (which is innate) and then tie it to biological sex (which we foolishly assume is binary) which leads us to allocate the same binary attributes to gender that we assign to sex. Thus, our social roles get inextricably braided into our sex and our identities in a way that makes separating them all out from each other impossible.

Gender critical feminists are obsessed by the hierarchical struggle between sex and gender, claiming that they're being bullied into accepting a contradictory idea that is logically incompatible with factual truth. If gender starts to supersede sex, so the thinking goes, society gets coerced into a form of doublethink. The problem with this Orwellian theory is that doublethink is enforced by newspeak, a deliberate simplification of language designed to dull the mind into compliance. This is a gross misrepresentation of what we're trying to do. On the contrary, our aim is to expand language to encompass a greater number of realities, to broaden the way we talk and think about sex and gender so that it becomes more truthful, not less. Dictionaries are growing bigger, not smaller, and while I'm not saying trans people are responsible for this, I'm also not saying we're not.

Think of it this way: Maybe the language we have now is the newspeak of Orwell's dystopia, only we don't know it because our minds can't grasp the scope of the vocabulary we'll be using in the future. What if all we do from here is expand?

✢ ✢ ✢

The claim that gender is socially constructed
has rung hollow for decades not because it isn't true,
but because it's wildly incomplete.

Andrea Long Chu

One of the earliest descriptions of a trans person was recorded in 1966 by Harry Benjamin in *The Transsexual Phenomenon:* "Their anatomical sex, that is to say, the body, is male. Their psychological sex, that is to say, the mind, is female."

Thus, he neatly cleaved us in half: mind and body, spirit and flesh. Gender becomes cerebral, intellectual, an ideology, a theory, an esoteric, unprovable substance trapped inside the scientifically verifiable mass called our sex.

Once upon a time I believed in gender too. I claimed that I had a brain that believed my body was male. It helped me to understand that if I couldn't change my mind to match my body, then I'd have to change my body to match my mind. It was a step I needed to take in my own evolution. Sometimes simplicity is necessary.

But the linguistic split between mind and body — invisible and visible — is part of the problem. We can make the claim that gender exists in the brain — that it is psychological — but the brain is part of the body. The neurons that fire around my brain are generated by my body, they are of my body, they cannot be separated from me. My gender is neither outside of me like an ideology, nor trapped inside as some spirit-like substance; it's not encased within my skin, there's no trapdoor to open, it can't escape. I am my body, I am only my body, my body is all the "I" that I am.

This is the sort of statement gender critical feminists would have a field day with. If I am only my body, and my body bears all the hallmarks of the female sex, how can I not be a woman? But this is precisely the point at which language fails us.

The way I wanted to describe how I felt pre-transition didn't make sense to anyone, least of all me: *I am a man, but something is wrong with my body.*

This had nothing to do with gender. Or if it did, this single word on its own was wholly incapable of describing the complexity of my experience.

Maybe one day, when scientists can adequately explain how the human brain creates consciousness, we will have better words to describe the experience of being trans. But for now, you will just have to trust that I am telling you the truth of how it feels for me.

"Sex is real" is the rallying cry of the gender critical feminists, and on this point, we are entirely in agreement. If our bodies didn't matter, we wouldn't go to such lengths to change them. What I dispute is the idea that sex is immutable. My body used to bear all the characteristics of the female sex, but my sex is not female, my sex is male. Using surgery and hormones to modify those characteristics was a gamble — I had no proof it was going to work other than my own intuition, my sense of self — but it paid off. After I changed my body, I was unquestionably the right sex. And only once I was the right sex could I look back and properly understand the wrongness of the sex that my body had formerly been. But this process was all in my body, a somatic experience governed by an instinct I still can't name.

I don't feel like I've changed sex. I know this is how it appears to other people, but it isn't how it feels to me. I have evolved my body to align it with the sex that I am. I have changed my body to become itself. I have affirmed my existing sex. We can use the word "transition" to try to explain this process, but I didn't transition from woman to man, because I was never a woman in the first place. So really, it's just a device to try to explain the inexplicable. Because how can my sex be misaligned with my sex? There must be something wrong with the available vocabulary.

I'll use the word "transition" to describe this experience of social and physical realignment in the pages of this book because it's the culturally agreed-upon term, but I want to state my discomfort with it.

My story requires new language, my body demands a new text.

✝ ✝ ✝

Gender identity is an oxymoron. Or a tautology. Or a redundant phrase. I'm not sure which.

For a start, nobody really understands what gender is. (At least, Judith Butler apparently understands what gender is, but since nobody understands Judith Butler, that's not much help.) Tomes have been written on the subject, the world's most brilliant minds have pondered the question, philosophers have been debating the matter since the time of Aristotle and Plato, and we're still no closer to a definitive answer upon which we can all agree. We can speculate, argue, guess, hypothesize, theorize or make strident claims, but ultimately gender remains a mystery.

Maybe gender is just another word for identity. But asking, *What is identity?* is like asking, *What is freedom?* As Nina Simone once pointed out, some things are impossible to describe. *It's just a feeling. It's just a feeling. It's like, how do you tell someone how it feels to be in love? How are you going to tell anybody who has not been in love, how it feels to be in love? You cannot do it to save your life.*

I can't tell you what my identity is, but I can sure as hell tell you what it's not. It's not a subjective belief system. Neither is it an ideology, a political statement, a marketing strategy, a token character, a book genre, a PR stunt, an act of rebellion, an aesthetic, an illusion, a religion, or a cult.

My identity is not separate from my body. My body is made up of physical matter which has been formatted in such a way that I have an experience which the dictionary calls gender dysphoria, which I have managed to overcome by doing what the dictionary calls transitioning. I am the literal definition of a trans man. If you have an argument with this, it's not with me, it's with the dictionary.

I stand in solidarity with the dictionary because I think it's become a bit of a scapegoat and I like to support the underdogs.

I first read my maleness in my fingernails, which have always been short and square like my father's. I used to try to feminize them — grow them long, cover them up with nail polish — but they remained defiantly male, a daily reminder that there was something amiss with the rest of my body.

My Adam's apple was easier to ignore, because I couldn't see it unless I was looking in a mirror. When I learned in biology class that women don't have Adam's apples, I didn't put up my hand and ask the teacher why I was the outlier to this rule. Anyway, nobody ever commented on my Adam's apple, probably because we don't spend much time looking at each other's throats. I just went through my life pretending it wasn't there.

Fingernails and an Adam's apple, breasts and a vagina. Two body parts for two body parts. Which of these do you choose as a statement of my sex?

I succumbed to the functionality of my sex organs. People told me what a vagina was for, so I used it that way; I allowed penises in and babies out. Now I call the erectile organ on the front of my pelvic bone a penis, but this isn't me trying to be clever. I don't call it a penis because it symbolizes masculinity, and I don't refuse to call it a clitoris as a rejection of femininity; I call it a penis because it is a penis. I know what the difference between a penis and a clitoris is, and I also know my own body.

This is not queer theory. This is my flesh and blood.

I also understand how insane this must sound to someone for whom clitoris and penis are two obviously different body parts with completely separate functions. But one person's insanity is another person's logic. "Far from the Internet where people rage about this issue," Grace Lavery says, "there is a group of women who find it utterly ridiculous that there is another group of women who go around asking questions like, *Can a woman have a penis?* When what they mean is, *Does the class 'woman' contain a subclass of women who have penises?*"

I belong to the subclass of men who have penises that are not visible to the human eye, or who have penises that are smaller than most, or who have penises that look like enlarged clitorises.

I would like to align my penis with other people's expectations, but this is expensive, complicated surgery. Only I can evaluate what I can live with and what needs to be changed. Only I know how far to go and where to stop.

Cis people navigate their bodies this way every day when they decide how to dress, what to eat, when to exercise, how to cut their hair, whether to get cosmetic surgery. We trans people just take our own steps, and some of them by necessity go further.

The problem with binary thinking is that it assumes that biological sex is immutable, that there are only two sexes, and that gender is a social construct. If there is no such thing as gender — only roles and expectations that are installed in our minds by society according to our biological sex — then if you don't like the role you've been ascribed, simply reject it and act or dress or behave in whichever way makes you feel happiest. This is exactly the kind of freedom I wish for everyone, but it's not a magical cure for dysphoria.

If we could accept that we each have our own individual identity that we need to outwardly portray on our bodies and remove the word "gender" from the whole equation, then perhaps we would get closer to the truth. If we allowed ourselves to understand sex as both profoundly important and also relatively elastic, then gender need no longer play a part. We could get rid of the word gender altogether.

Why is the idea of each of us owning a singular, uncategorized body so hard?

✢ ✢ ✢

If gender exists at all, maybe we should think of it as a gift; not in the metaphorical sense, but as a thing that is given. When gender is assigned, whether at birth or at any other stage of life, it becomes part of a transactional relationship.

Consider the person sitting in the coffee shop. She has short hair and is dressed in jeans, boots, and a shirt rolled up to the elbows. She is drinking a cup of coffee and reading the newspaper. She sits with her legs astride. She takes up space. When she interacts with the barista, she speaks with authority. She doesn't smile too much. She likes to mow the lawn, take out the garbage, drink beer, and have casual sex. She's the cliché of a man, but even taking all this into account, you look at the cluster of her visible physical attributes and you ascribe her a gender: Female.

Then consider the same person sitting in the same coffee shop after a few years on testosterone. Now he has a beard, and when he speaks to the barista, his voice is noticeably lower. Almost everything else is the same, but you give him a different gender: Male.

His identity hasn't changed. He has done what he needed to do with his body, and in return you gave him a different gender. It's a neat exchange, a transaction he's negotiated with you using the currency supplied by the society in which you both live. The visual cues are his bid, the allocation of gender is your response. Your acknowledgement of his gender is the gift you give him.

Sometimes people make mistakes; they give the wrong gift to the wrong person. It happens. If you find someone politely declining your gift, don't be upset. Just ask them what they would prefer and give them that instead. It's terribly easy to do and won't cost you a thing. Don't insist they take your gift just because you're certain they should have it. If you try to force a gift on someone who doesn't want it, you breach a boundary.

It doesn't matter how much someone might want to give me the female gender, I will not take it. If they don't accept my refusal, it becomes a consent issue. That's when gift-giving becomes an act of aggression.

I was given the wrong gender at birth. It took me decades to realize that I could give it back.

*Many trans and non-trans people alike are immersed
in a fiction: the fiction that they themselves, or others
around them, have literally changed sex.*

Kathleen Stock

I have been immersed in a fiction, but not the one you think.

I'm very familiar with the amount of work it takes to believe
something that is not true, because for several decades I indulged in
the fantasy that I was a woman. I never questioned why maintaining
this illusion took so much work, nor did I consciously acknowledge
that the scenario was fictional, because this would have broken the
immersive state. Everyone believed that I was a woman, so I believed
it too. We were all operating under a mass delusion.

If you, too, are a man, then try to imagine how this feels: Close
your eyes and imagine yourself wearing a dress and a pair of high
heels. Now imagine that you must wear these clothes every day. You
must put on lipstick and mascara every time you leave the house,
because you're afraid that if you don't, someone might notice that
you're a man. You want to blend in, but this means you must pay
attention to everything you do and everything you say for every
minute of every day, forever. You can never relax because if you do,
you'll probably do something wrong. You spend your life watching
other women so you can figure out what it is they're doing that makes
them seem feminine, and then you copy it. You learn how to move,
and how to sit, and how to hold your body so that you look like a
woman. You feel uncomfortable all the time, and you want to stop, but

you don't know how. You become so afraid of being found out that you start to become more womanly, not less, and the more womanly you become, the more distressed you feel. Your heels get higher, your makeup gets thicker, your jewelry gets heavier, you start to feel grotesque. You have panic attacks. You wake in the middle of the night with your heart racing. You become agoraphobic and stop wanting to leave the house. You would do anything to just take it all off and relax, but you can't, or you'll reveal the fact that you're a man, and then everyone will be horrified by you. You'll lose everything. Everyone will reject you. There's no way out.

The scene above can act as a litmus test for whether you prioritize sex or gender. If you think I'm describing a trans woman here, check your perspective. A trans woman finds comfort and pleasure in dressing as a woman, whereas I only found discomfort and distress. What I'm describing is the dysphoria of a trans man who is still trying to hide his true gender.

This is the life I led for 40 years. I know what it's like to be immersed in a fiction, and it takes work. Constant, endless, mind-fucking, body-breaking work.

Gender critical feminists say that we are immersing ourselves in a fiction to find relief from feelings of dysphoria, but this only proves that they have no idea what dysphoria is, or what generates it. The dysphoria is created by the cognitive dissonance required to maintain the fiction of our socially assigned gender. When we stop denying who we are, the dysphoria disappears.

Once I'd woken up to the fact that I was an adult human male, the rest was relatively easy.

3. Fences

I used to be afraid. Actually, I'm still afraid, it's just that my fears have changed. I used to be afraid of being gay, or being trans, or being male, or being myself in any way at all. Now I'm just afraid of Daniel Lavery.

I'm afraid of Daniel Lavery because we transitioned at the same time, but while I was doing it all by myself in private, Daniel was doing it in public with his wife. And because they were both talking and writing about it so openly — and because I was lonely and didn't know many other trans people at the time — Daniel and his wife Grace became my imaginary best friends.

Daniel and I can't be best friends in real life, obviously, because Daniel is completely out of my league. There are writers who write about being trans, and then there is Daniel Lavery. Reading Daniel's work (I cannot call him Danny like everyone else does, so don't ask me to) feels a little like having your spinal cord wired directly into the Hadron Collider. His humor is so sharp that it's hard to believe he's not British (his wife is, so that may account for some of it) and he doesn't tolerate fools. Write something stupid about being trans and Daniel will dismiss you with a flick of his pen, and he'll do it with such wit, such ruthless satire, such merciless panache that you won't even know what happened. I wake up every morning and pray that Daniel never reads a word I write. Everyone else can be as mean as they like — I don't care — but I don't want Daniel Lavery to spurn me because he was once my imaginary best friend and I love him too much.

Anyway, this fear is very specific, and has nothing at all to do with the fears that keep cis people and trans people from having useful conversations with each other. Because before we can talk about what cisgender people deserve to hear — and how we can give it to you — we need to talk about what's getting in the way.

✛ ✛ ✛

Once upon a time I was in a relationship with a woman who liked fences.

The women were fenced off in this one field over here, and the men were fenced off in that other field over there. Because I grew up in the English countryside, I pictured them like two fields of sheep, quietly chomping on the grass, occasionally coming up against a nice wooden post, having a quick back scratch and then wandering off again. This is our binary world, where the two sexes are separated off from each other. There is no migration, there are no gates between the fields, and the fences never move. It's all quite tidy and controlled.

In each field, there are rules. Even if you're unhappy with the rules, there is still a certain security in knowing which field you're in and who you're fighting against. Your enemy is clearly visible in the other field, and you are clearly visible to them. The fences remain intact, because regardless of what anyone thinks about the rules themselves — who is afforded what status, who holds the power — at least everyone agrees about who belongs in which field. Binaries are simple like that.

Until trans people came along.

Because trans bodies can't be contained. They are slippery and liquid, they move invisibly between the fields, and that frightens people. So they call us sneaky and undermining, they accuse us of going by stealth, disguised and undercover. They say we are unpredictable and dishonorable, that we change our minds, switch allegiance or desert the fight altogether. They cannot allow this to continue. It's anarchy. The biological men must remain on one side of the fence, and the biological women must remain on the other.

But why?

I once woke up in the middle of the night with the thought: Why do there have to be any fences in the first place? Why can't we just have full run of the countryside? In my half-asleep dream-state this seemed like a very reasonable question, one I momentarily couldn't answer. Seriously, if we live in a democratic society, why should anyone have to give a reason for wanting to be whichever sex or gender they happened to feel like being? Why don't we all have free choice on this matter? This isn't just about trans people; it is about everyone. Why in god's name are we not all allowed to be whoever the hell we like?

But then the world came back into focus, and I remembered that the problem, of course, was the propensity of Western humans to hold an innate bias against the feminine. While it had been relatively easy for me to reject femininity and embrace masculinity, it hadn't been so easy for those of my friends who wanted to do the reverse. Even if we broke down all the fences, the stigma surrounding "choosing femininity" would still remain, which means we can't truly be free until we can rid everyone in the world of the idea that one gender is better than the other.

It's misogyny, stupid.

✛ ✛ ✛

Margaret Atwood believes that stories are what hold nation-states together; that if one story falls apart and it's not replaced by another, fragmentation is the result. *You have the first generation who were the fervent utopianists ... and then you win, and then what do you do when you win? What's supposed to happen is the golden age is supposed to appear. Then it doesn't appear. Then what? Well, you've won and you've eliminated your enemies, your original enemies. But it's still not working. So it must be a betrayal from within ...*

The feminist origin story — vastly simplified — is one where women are good and men are bad, and the good and the bad exist in two separate camps. The bad camp holds all the power, and the good camp wants to pull that power over the fence into their camp. Few feminists today hold such rigid views, but the ones who still do believe that good can only win if bad loses. It's a story as old as time — the zero-sum game — but it only works if the sex of the individual players doesn't change.

This desire to separate us out — whether in restrooms or prisons or sports teams — stems from a fear for the safety of the female body. I'm not saying the fear itself is illegitimate, I'm just saying it has nothing to do with trans people.

Trans people have become the focus of this fear partly because we represent the threat of betrayal from within. How, exactly, do you fence out the trans people? Particularly the ones who pass, because if we pass, we disappear from view, which means we can just slip back in again. God forbid we should be allowed to change our gender markers all the way back to our birth certificates, because if we do, *how is anyone ever going to know we're trans?* No wonder we're creating a moral panic.

But trans people are not inherently dangerous. The assumption that we're dangerous is rooted in your subconscious: it's a phobia, an anxiety disorder defined by a persistent and excessive fear of an object. Of course, you'll find examples of bad players if you search hard enough, but this is true of any community, and "some trans women are dangerous, therefore all trans women must be excluded" is not a benign position to take.

Individual people are dangerous. Systems of oppression are dangerous. Trans people, as a group, are not.

The solution is not to fence us out, but to get over the fear.

✦ ✦ ✦

There is no sex. There is but sex that is oppressed and sex that oppresses. It is oppression that creates sex and not the contrary.

Monique Wittig

It is clearly untrue that all people with penises want to oppress women, and equally as untrue that all people with uteruses want to fight that oppression. If we must have a fence, wouldn't it be more sensible to place it between those who want to the uphold the patriarchal system and those who want to dismantle it?

The irony is that cis women and trans people all have the same fear: for our safety and for our bodily autonomy. The enemy is not men, or masculinity, or penises, or testosterone; the enemy is misogyny. But while the symptoms of misogyny are real, misogyny itself is an ideology based on a socially constructed hierarchy. And hierarchical structures are like money; they only work if everyone believes in them.

Take me and my friend Phoebe as an example. Phoebe, who is a woman, used to be a father, while I, who am a man, used to be a mother. We are each other's fiercest allies, but whereas previously Phoebe would have taken a stand to protect me against misogyny, now I have to stand up to protect her. This switch in roles implies a switch in power, but neither Phoebe nor I have changed as people; she is not weaker than she used to be when she presented as a man, and I am not stronger than I was when I presented as a woman. We are just being treated differently, because in the eyes of the public we have each moved across the fence. I have been given more authority, while she has had hers taken away.

Trans people are the ultimate proof that the gender hierarchy is all in our minds. Or in other people's minds, anyway.

Ta-Nehisi Coates summed this up nicely while talking about race: *The power of domination and exclusion is central to the belief in being white, and without it, "white people" would cease to exist for want of reasons.*

So perhaps there is something to the gender critical claim that nobody is trans. Because if cis people only exist in relation to trans people, then if nobody is trans, nobody is cis either. And if cis people don't exist, then that means that neither gender nor sex is real. And if neither gender nor sex is real then probably everyone is trans.

This is all intentional nonsense of course, but that's the point.

✝ ✝ ✝

Depending on your sources, there are currently between 72 and 93 different gender identities out there to choose from. The common response to this statement is an eyeroll followed by a disparaging comment about the self-indulgence of queer youth. *Why do we need so many genders? What's the point?*

There are eight billion people on this earth, and we use over 750 million first names to identify each person. We accept this nomenclative diversity as normal but imagine if we didn't. Imagine if everyone in the world was called either Bill or Jane. We are perfectly comfortable using wildly expansive ways to describe who we are and what we believe in and how we think and what we do, and yet we still try to constrain ourselves to two choices when describing something as critical to our identities as sex and gender. This is what I mean when I say that in some areas of our language, we are already Orwellian. The potential expansiveness of our imaginations is being suffocated by the restrictions of our language.

But where does it all end? I hear you cry. *How are we supposed to remember who is what?*

Look, I'm not great with names. Seconds after being introduced to a new person I'll remember the strength of their handshake, the tone of their voice, and the general vibe of their energy, but their name will already have flown from my mind. If everyone was called Bill or Jane it would make my life so much easier, but this would mean asking everyone else to accommodate my shortcoming. It's my problem to fix, not theirs. If we accept that it's not self-indulgent to have individual names, why can't we do the same with gender? I get that broadening our choices makes life more complicated, but isn't the expansion of knowledge and understanding the *raison d'être* of the human race?

Imagine a world where you could be a Bill or a Jane if you wanted to be, or something else entirely if you didn't. A world where Bill and Jane weren't the norms from which we deviate, but just two of many choices. In a world like this, isn't it possible that all the Bills and Janes out there might start wondering whether they might perhaps be something a little more interesting than merely a Bill or a Jane? Might they not want to explore other options? Don't you think they might find that a little bit exciting?

We are assigned a name at birth, one in a choice of millions, and a gender, one in a choice of two. It just seems a little unimaginative.

Identities are unique, like personalities. We accept that personalities are made up of millions of different patterns of thoughts, feelings, and behaviors that distinguish each person from the next; some are genetic, and others socialized, some deeply rooted and others more fluid. We don't split people into two personality types, ask everyone to conform to either one or the other, and then punish the people who can't. That would be insane. So why do we do this with identities?

And yet I don't underestimate the degree to which belonging to a sex-based class can make a person feel secure. When I first started to question my gender, I felt like a fully assembled Lego spaceship that had come apart in zero gravity, like all my little Lego pieces were spinning around in outer space, unattached to anything and totally formless. This is not a very comfortable condition to find oneself in, and I can't imagine many people who would voluntarily enter this destabilized state without feeling a very compelling need to do so.

In *The Fire Next Time* James Baldwin pointed out that the white man *"is in sore need of new standards, which will release him from his confusion and place him once again in fruitful communion with the depths of his own being."*

Fruitful communion with the depths of one's own being can be a very frightening thing to engage in. Trust me, I've been there.

And yet the lasting freedom is worth the temporary discomfort.

I reframe the crisis of anti-trans violence as having actually nothing to do with trans people, it has to do with non-trans people who don't know their own embodiment, their own spiritual being outside of the costumes they've been fitted into, predetermined without their choice.

Alok Vaid-Menon

If white people can listen to James Baldwin, maybe more cis people can start listening to Alok.

What does it take to wake up to the fact that the life you've been living was designed by someone else? What if you don't feel a compelling need to wake up? Or what if your happiness depends on you not waking up? This isn't a new question for trans people — we've all seen *The Matrix* — but sometimes we forget that the questions we ask of ourselves are not necessarily the same ones being asked by everyone else.

Sometimes, when I feel the shame of my colonial past, I wonder what would have happened if my gender identity and sexual orientation hadn't forced me out of my safe, white bubble. Would I still be the person I was before I read Baldwin, before I managed to divest myself of the notion that I was *"in possession of some intrinsic value that black people need or want"*? Would I have understood that hierarchies of power only exist through separation, and that fences preserve these structures? I believed that being trans was lesser, that the gold standard was to be cis. It took a lot to blow that idea apart.

But sometimes it's only by coming apart completely that we can put ourselves back together in a shape that feels entirely our own, rather than one copied from the back of the Lego box. Trans people are forced to throw away the instruction manual and start from scratch. Humans come in an infinite combination of different pieces. Trans people simply embrace this fact.

I know it's overwhelming to imagine that there might be millions of variations of cis, trans and nonbinary people out there, and each of us needs to be treated as an individual, and all of us should be equally free. It feels chaotic, uncontrollable. But when in god's name was the human race ever simple? We have words for the type of people who want to control humanity, and they're not usually flattering.

We have to question our preference for structure over content, for simplicity over complexity, for control over freedom.

The problem is reductionism. The solution is complex thinking. And no fences.

4. Procreation

We can recognize that this impacts women while also
recognizing that it impacts other groups. Those things
are not mutually exclusive, Senator Hawley.

Khiara Bridges

People who menstruate. Bodies with vaginas. Six emotionally explosive words.

The last time I went for an OB GYN appointment, I'd grown a beard. When I checked in at the front desk, I just gave them my name, Oliver Radclyffe, because I'd learned by this point that unnecessary explanations tend to embarrass people. I handed them my insurance card and was given the relevant paperwork to sign. None of the pregnant women in the waiting room took very much notice of me. The nurse who led me through into the inner sanctum was new, so I thought it might be helpful to give her some relevant information. "I'm trans," I said, as I stepped onto the scale. "Yes," she replied, as if to say, *Well, obviously. You have a uterus and a beard.*

After my examination, I didn't stop on my way back out through the waiting room to ask any of the pregnant women their thoughts on having to share a gynecological office with a man, but I'm fairly certain none of them considered me a threat to their womanhood. My presence had no impact on their identities; they were women before I arrived, and they were women after I left. At most I'd given them the opportunity to spot a bona-fide trans man in the wild, a rare sighting which they could tell their friends about over brunch the next day.

Beyond that, it was a perfectly normal day for all of us, and we all got through it with our identities and our rights intact.

This is not a very interesting story because there was neither conflict nor resolution. There was no hostility, no interrogation, not even much awkwardness; I was made to feel as safe and welcome after my transition as I had been before. Was this because my OB GYN had excised the word "woman" from all their literature and replaced it with "people with uteruses"? Probably not. As far as I was aware the word "woman" was still available on their website, but the truth was I had no idea, because I hadn't bothered to check.

I'm not an idiot, and contrary to what gender critical feminists would have you believe, neither are most trans people. We do understand that the majority of people with uteruses are women. It's nice when an organization or an advertising campaign or — in the most frequently cited case — a British medical journal acknowledges that trans men and nonbinary folk can give birth, but honestly what matters to us most is our safety and our dignity, access to necessary resources, and being made to feel like legitimate human beings while our cervixes are going through their annual wellness checks.

It is, of course, tempting to point out that the collective noun "people" makes no mention of sex or gender and therefore dehumanizes and excludes nobody, but indulging in a game of etymological ping-pong diverts us from the fact that the gender critical feminists are trying to persuade everyone that trans activists want to erase women by removing the word "woman" from, well, everywhere, apparently. We don't. The assertion is absurd; our whole ethos is based on wanting everyone to identify as exactly who and what they are. But when this message becomes so pervasive that even the *New York Times* is publishing opinion pieces that claim we're trying to shove women to the side — to reduce them to their body parts, reinforce outdated gender stereotypes, deny them the right to call themselves women, and ultimately shut them up — we have to ask ourselves why.

Either what we're saying is being badly misunderstood, or it's being willingly misinterpreted.

Imagine a scene half a million years ago. A man is out hunting wildebeests while his mate is stuck at home in the cave, breastfeeding their child. The sperm-producing man is assigned more power than his egg-producing partner because he has the freedom to leave the cave, thus we end up with a social hierarchy where two different groups are assigned lesser or greater status based on their reproductive organs.

This is obviously a vastly simplified account of the origins of sex-based hierarchy, but it serves as a reminder that the Western binary system was generated by humans who were almost certainly not aware of the existence of trans people. Which means that now we have become visible, there's nowhere for us to go. We need to consider that either the two-field system is wrong, or trans people are wrong. And given that trans people are human beings and therefore cannot be "wrong" in any moral or practical sense of the word, perhaps we ought to assume that the problem lies with the system— the fields and fences.

What would happen if we broke down the fence between the two procreators, now that the material basis for the idea that one is stronger than the other has disappeared? Stopped focusing on which body was producing the sperm or the egg, and assumed equal freedom and shared responsibility for both partners? Isn't this one of the fundamental aims of feminism?

Any feminist serious about dismantling patriarchal privilege should embrace the trans movement, because for us the production of sperm or egg is no longer immutably twinned with either sex, so we demonstrably undo the basis for the status belief in the present moment. Which explains why so many people get so upset about the idea of a pregnant trans man, or a trans woman with a penis. It screws with an age-old belief system in a way that feels wildly uncomfortable, even to someone who categorically wants to undo the hierarchical structures that that belief system created.

The mythical hierarchy of female weakness / inferiority and male strength / superiority can only exist if the two sexes remain separate. Keep the fences, and the hierarchy self-perpetuates. Break down the fences and the hierarchy disappears.

Isn't this the easiest way to overthrow the patriarchy?

It's just a thought.

✛ ✛ ✛

Because of gender identity ideology, the quest for the
liberation of people with female bodies has arrived at
an extraordinary position: that they do not even constitute
a group that merits a name.

Helen Joyce

This might be a good moment to repeat that as far as I'm aware nobody
in the trans movement is trying to get rid of women. Asking you
to imagine a fenceless society is merely an invitation to indulge in
a theoretical exercise in self-liberation from socially constructed
narratives. It's not a recruitment into a totalitarian ideological
movement hellbent on violently enforcing gender fluidity.

Also, trans men are not trying to opt out of oppression, and
therefore — by default — out of the feminist movement. In the early
days of feminism, to be equal meant to be "just like a man" but we've
moved beyond that now, and anyone who thinks this is what trans
men are trying to do is entirely mistaken. We're not trying to be like
men, we are men. Moreover, we're fully aware that many people have
no desire to be "just like a man," including quite a few men themselves.
To be equal is to be equally free to choose how we identify, dress,
behave, learn, work, speak, build, procreate, and love, irrespective of
gender. The only people trans people want to be "like" are themselves.

The gender critical feminist Helen Joyce makes much of the
recent rise in numbers of teenage trans boys and nonbinary people
who are questioning their gender identities, compared to the lower
numbers of trans girls. She likens our gender dysphoria to "historical

episodes of mass hysteria, such as fainting fits, uncontrollable laughter or crying, outbreaks of paralysis or tremors." She's using this rhetoric as a form of control, to linguistically slap us out of our delusions. It's the oldest game in the book. She's using shame to try to get us to stay inside the fence.

But the rise in numbers of trans-masculine adolescents merely speaks to the fact that it's more socially acceptable to move toward a masculine presentation than a feminine one. Helen has tried to convince herself that the degree to which we succumb to our dysphoria — whether we try to suppress it or give in and modify our bodies — is culturally determined; that our trans identities are dictated by external influences. But it's not our identities that respond to external influences, it's the degree to which we're willing to reveal ourselves. There aren't fewer trans-female adolescents, they're simply more afraid of coming out.

It's misogyny again. And Helen — an alleged feminist — is playing into it.

✢ ✢ ✢

I see this conversation as an extension of the pro-life argument. We are not talking about the life of the child, but we are talking about the potential to give life to another generation.

Idaho State Rep. Julianne Young

An oft-quoted side effect of taking testosterone is that it leads to dry vagina and problems lactating. No matter that the trans man in question might not want to be penetrated or to breast feed, because according to the evangelicals the needs of the trans man are not paramount in this conversation. All they can see is the ruination of the female body designed by God for the use of man.

In recent years breast augmentation has outweighed chest masculinization as a surgical choice for teenagers by roughly four to one, and yet nobody's trying to pass legislation to prevent teenage girls from getting their breasts enlarged. This may, of course, have something to do with who benefits from that surgery. Arguably, chest masculinization might be one of the few cosmetic procedures that is performed solely to satisfy the gaze of the person who owns the body.

But maybe the fear runs deeper than the concern that women might stop taking men's desires into consideration when they make decisions about their bodies.

The categories of man and woman underpin those of father and mother, and the relationship of each to their children. If such categories are to become a matter of self-declaration, then those ties must be dissolved.

Helen Joyce

Here's how it's supposed to go: Men work hard to build their careers and for that they are rewarded with a beautiful wife who will provide them with a happy home and adoring children. *But it's my turn!* we hear the men cry plaintively as they watch their women desert them for other women, or refuse to have babies, or steal their jobs, or transition into men. But maybe there's more going on here, maybe it's more existential than that. There's clearly a link between the opposition to gay marriage, the pro-life movement, the policing of female bodies, and transphobia. Could it be a fundamental fear that humans will die out if women aren't forced to procreate?

Because seriously. How does procreation work with trans people? Who carries the baby? Are they even fertile? How does trans sex happen? What goes where? How can the sperm ever hope to meet the egg if everyone's reproductive bits have been messed around with? And we're not even getting started on who's supposed to be called what, or which role each person is supposed to play.

Surely this is the end of civilization as we know it?

Trans people can't be parents. It's just too confusing. And yet some of us are. Quite successfully, if I may say so myself.

I slept with men and then I slept with women and neither of those choices had any impact on whether I wanted to be a parent. I was a mother and now I am a father and neither of those definitions had any impact on how I parented my children. People who want to have children will go on having them, and people who don't, won't. The human race may not survive, but if it doesn't, it almost certainly won't be the fault of trans people.

5. Second Act

One evening in the early 1990s, long before I realized I was trans —
or even, for that matter, attracted to women — I went with some
friends to see the comedian Suzy Izzard perform live at a theater
in London. I didn't know Suzy was trans back then. I thought, like
everyone else, that she was just a man who liked wearing make-up.

Strutting around the stage in a pair of jeans teamed with high
heels, nail polish and red lipstick, Suzy made me laugh until I cried
with her unique brand of surreal humor. At the end of the show, I
asked my friends to wait for me at the front of the theater while I ran
around the corner to the restaurant where we'd eaten dinner earlier
that evening. I grabbed the flowers that had been sitting in a vase
on our table, and then ran back to the theater's backstage entrance.
When Suzy appeared through the door, I thrust out the flowers and
said, *these are for you.*

What Suzy made of being accosted by a young girl in her early
twenties holding a dripping wet bunch of flowers that had clearly just
been pulled out of a vase, I have no idea, but she was gracious, if not
exactly overwhelmed. She handed the flowers to her backstage
manager and then got into the car that was waiting for her and drove
away, leaving me standing awkwardly on the sidewalk trying to make
sense of my emotions. I had no clue what I was feeling, all I knew was
that I'd never felt it before, and I'd needed to do something about it —
take some kind of definitive action — and this was all I'd been able to
come up with at short notice.

For years afterwards I felt stupid and embarrassed, not understanding what had compelled me to make such an uncharacteristically
dramatic gesture, but when we both finally transitioned everything

seemed to make sense. Of course, I'd wanted to give Suzy flowers, because despite all evidence to the contrary, she was a woman, and I was a man.

This is a cute little story because it contains all the necessary ingredients — complication, action and resolution — and the final reveal is so satisfyingly neat and tidy. But Suzy's identity is not as simple as this version of the story makes out, and as I read years later in her memoir, my gesture was neither as original nor as charming as I'd hoped it would be.

Because I am transgender, people buy me flowers, and when they do I say to them, "I don't know what to do with the flowers." I say, "Thank you for the flowers, but do you want to keep them? Or do you want them back? Because you can have them back if you want." I can do flowers if someone puts them in a vase. Flowers are great in a vase; they do look bright and colorful — which means I can appreciate them. But when people send flowers or give me flowers, loose flowers, flowers in a bunch, that are now in my hand, I just go, "I don't know what to do with this." Believe Me: A Memoir of Love, Death, and Jazz Chickens (2017)

Obviously, the punchline is that I should have stolen the bloody vase as well, but the point is that from a trans perspective this story doesn't have such a clear narrative after all. It's true that when Suzy walked out on stage, I'd felt instinctively that she was female — despite the fact that she wasn't yet publicly identifying as such — and in recognizing her, I also recognized myself, but this feeling of recognition was more complex than the anecdote can encompass. The narrative of my trans identity didn't start with me giving Suzy flowers, and it didn't end with Suzy coming out as a trans woman. There was no "big reveal" for either of us, we just grew into our identities slowly, in the gradual, non-linear way that trans people do.

Cis people like a big reveal because it signals the point of change, a recognizable moment when the trans person moves from the "before" gender to the "after," but as I've mentioned before, this isn't generally how transitions work. And even if it were, we still wouldn't be able to control which part of our transition is the part that magically shifts the public's perception of us. Suzy first revealed her identity to the British press back in 1991, but because she refused to stick to the approved script, nobody took much notice. All the terms that made perfect sense to her — *action transvestite, complete-boy-plus-half-girl, lesbian trapped in a man's body, total clothing rights advocate* — made little sense to the wider world, so her presentation was dismissed as quirky, performative, and just part of the show.

It wasn't until 2020 that Suzy's identity became concrete in the minds of the cisgender public, when she casually announced during a brief television appearance that she preferred she / her pronouns. The media immediately framed it as an announcement of her trans identity, which must have come as a bit of a surprise to Suzy given that she'd been identifying that way for almost 30 years. *It's not like it came out of the blue,* she said. But for a lot of people, it did.

So, what changed?

It's easy to assume that public recognition of Suzy as a trans woman came about because she adopted new pronouns, but for the pronouns themselves to have had such an effect, the public must first have learned to read the message that was being sent. And the fact that they were able to understand that message was the direct result of a sea change in the public's awareness around trans issues which started to occur sometime during the early 2000s.

There is a common misconception that trans people are new, but of course this is not true. Trans people have always existed, and not in the tiny numbers everyone assumes. Trans historians have managed to dig out a few examples of gender-nonconforming figures from the past, but highlighting these rare examples leads to the false impression that they were the only trans people who existed back then. The frustrating by-product of using invisibility as a survival tactic is that we leave little trace of ourselves for other people to find, which adds to the mistaken belief that we're a relatively new and rare phenomenon.

I don't want to alarm anyone, but just because you couldn't see us didn't mean we weren't there.

Invisibility comes in many forms and is worn for many reasons. I was invisible pre-transition because I wanted everyone to believe I was a girl; Suzy was invisible because nobody understood the terms she was using to describe herself. It's almost as if people are unable to see the trans identity until it's defined by a specific collection of attributes, ones that are unique to only a tiny proportion of trans people. If you had suffered terribly as a child, overcome seemingly insurmountable obstacles to transition, and had then adopted a brand new, binary gender, you were trans. If you didn't fit this narrative, you weren't.

This enabled the cis public to acknowledge the existence of a token handful of trans people without having to worry that one day there might be too many of us to manage. Of course, the vast majority of trans people don't fit this narrative, and even if they did, we'd rather not have to classify ourselves as "suffering individuals" in order to get the treatment we need. Being trans shouldn't require us to have tremendous courage, and suffering certainly shouldn't be the first word that comes to mind when you think of us. We are — oh my god — so much more than that.

But while our identities may have been hidden from the general public, they were rarely hidden from each other. The connection that forms between trans people sometimes feels like the mycorrhizal network that runs between the roots of trees; it's a symbiotic relationship that exists beneath the ground, something we can't always see but can instinctively feel. It's like having some kind of subcutaneous sixth sense. Trans people don't require certainty from each other; on the contrary, we're usually slightly suspicious of anyone who claims to know exactly who or what they are. Curiosity is our calling card, and ambiguity comes with the territory.

We recognize each other not because any of us claim to have figured out the answers, but because we're all asking the same kinds of questions.

✛ ✛ ✛

In his book *The Quiet Before,* Gal Beckerman suggests that every revolution is preceded by a period of incubation during which the invisible army gathers its strength. While I'm not sure that the trans community was as organized as this makes us sound, with the benefit of hindsight it does seem that many of us had been part of a wave that had been growing in size and velocity for a number of years, one that started to crest around the year that *TIME* magazine put Laverne Cox on its cover.

There's no question that the internet was instrumental in this. The early 2000s introduced Facebook, then YouTube, then Twitter, and then Instagram, which meant that all the individual drops of energy gathering strength in the ocean could find each other, spread the word and rise up together. But the speed and volume at which the wave broke, flooding the world with trans people, created a backlash that was unavoidable.

Saul Alinsky, a 1970s community organizer quoted by Beckerman, suggested that a successful revolution should follow the structure of a three-act play: *The first act introduces the characters and the plot, in the second act the plot and characters are developed as the play strives to hold the audience's attention. In the final act good and evil have their dramatic confrontation and resolution.* But in a culture where the internet and social media can now disseminate massive quantities of new information at great speed, the characters in the second act of the play barely have time to engage with their audience before they're thrust into full confrontation with their enemies. And without the empathy of the audience, their chances of survival are badly compromised.

We can't blame the internet for this because the internet is our friend — it gave us a way to come together when it was unsafe to step out in public — and we can't blame ourselves, since for those of us whose lives hung in the balance, time wasn't a luxury we could afford.

We needed to come out *en masse*, and there was no way to do it quietly. But we barely got past, *Hi, my name is* ... before our adversaries pushed us straight into the third act, in the hope that they could get rid of us before we said anything that people might find interesting. So, none of you had the chance to get to know us before you were asked to decide whether or not you thought we should be allowed to exist.

How are you supposed to form an opinion with so little information? Where are you supposed to get your information from when you don't know which questions you're allowed to ask? No wonder so many of you just want to avoid the subject altogether.

But we've sent our bravest — the attorneys, the advocates and the activists — out to the front lines to fight the enemy, so you don't need to go there straight away. Pause for a moment, give yourself time to look around. If you step away from the heat of the battle, you'll see that our second act is happening right now, all around you. Our adversaries want to keep you focused on the fight-to-the-death stuff because they don't want you to notice the other stuff we're doing that you might actually enjoy. So, you'll have to consciously tune them out, turn the dial on the radio until you can only hear us instead.

Because we're all out here doing our thing, waiting for you to notice us, just like Suzy, who quietly broke down a shit-ton of boundaries before people caught up with what she was doing. We're publishing essays, writing books, and slamming poetry; we're hosting podcasts, making music, and performing comedy; we're producing movies, acting in television shows, and staging plays. Some of us — like myself — are new; others of us — like Suzy — have been doing this for decades.

But we're having a party out beyond the fences, and everyone's invited. You'll find none of the fanatical authoritarianism we're being accused of out here; fluidity is our hallmark, the freedom to be uncertain, to question, to change our minds. Doubt is the antidote to dogma and show me a trans person whose art hasn't sprung from an unmade bed of insatiable curiosity.

Of course, you'll also find us in the less performative spaces if you look hard enough. We are serving your food, and fixing your cars, and working in your hospitals, and writing your code; we are your best friend's daughter, or your babysitter's uncle, or your hairdresser's sister, or your grandchild's future. The quieter ones amongst us have just as much to tell you, but only if you're willing to show an interest, ask us questions, and listen to what we are trying to say.

And don't just listen the first one of us you happen to meet. One person cannot represent our entire community; we're far too diverse to be reduced to a single experience. You'll only understand the freedom we have when you realize how much we celebrate each other's differences, how we see each person's individuality as their strength. This is the kind of freedom we want to share with you, the kind of joy we want to bring more of into the world.

Why rely on someone else to tell you what to think about us when you can form your own opinion? We are doing our best to talk to you, and it's up to you to choose whether you listen to us — the only people who can tell you the truth about our lives — or to the people who want us gone.

6. The Future

*So many people think a positive outcome for a trans kid
is becoming cis. Not only is it not possible to make a
trans kid cis, being trans is such a gift. So if we are your
nightmare of who your kid can grow up to be, you don't
understand our magic at all.*

Chase Strangio

When I made the decision to start transitioning, I changed therapists.
I loved my previous therapist with all my heart, but eight years
previously I'd said to him, *I think I'm trans,* and he replied, *I don't
think you are,* and after that we just never revisited the subject.
Every time I worried about it, I reassured myself that my therapist
had insisted I wasn't trans and he'd probably know, right? Well, no,
firstly because he hadn't insisted on anything, and secondly because
my therapist, bless him, was a straight, cisgender man. A very kind
and thoughtful and intelligent straight, cisgender man, to be sure, but
still. This wasn't really his territory.

I found a new therapist, one who used they / them pronouns
but declined to tell me anything else about their identity because
they didn't want to influence who I might become. They had an
office in Brooklyn opposite a French patisserie that sold the best
pain au chocolat I'd tasted outside of France, and they were extremely
gentle with me when I showed up on their sofa surrounded by my
house-wrecking tornado of despair. *I don't know what I am,* I said, as
we both ducked to avoid a whirling tree branch. *I'm completely coming
apart,* I told them as a section of roof narrowly missed scalping us

both. *I belong to nobody and nothing,* I wailed as a cow whistled past. My new therapist sat with me calmly while the storm raged around the room. They'd seen it all before.

When the storm died down, my new therapist started asking me questions. They did not ask me when I'd first known, or whether I'd ever secretly dressed up in my father's suits, or whether I'd thrown a tantrum every time someone made me put on a dress. They never even mentioned the colors pink or blue. My new therapist is not an idiot.

My new therapist wanted to help me find out who I was, so we talked about what made me happy and what made me anxious, what gave me pleasure and what made me dissociate, what made me feel like myself and what made me feel like someone I thought I was supposed to be. They did not demand that I reduce myself to gender stereotypes or body parts, nor did they require me to fit into some prefabricated trans template. It was a long, slow, gentle, kind, unhurried exploration, performed with neither judgement nor expectation, during which I gradually peeled away all the stuff that wasn't me until I could find the real person underneath.

Remember how I said I wished the "suffering" part could be removed from the trans experience? If I'd had access to a therapist like this when I was a child, that might have been possible.

Contrary to what gender critical feminists, right-wing Republicans, and evangelical Christians would have you believe, gender therapists do not want their patients to change gender. Gender therapists want their patients to uncover their *existing* gender, whatever that may be. There is no agenda to this gender exploration beyond greater self-knowledge, and what you do with that self-knowledge is then very much up to you.

I could've bought a strap-on and returned to my life as a lesbian. I could've thrown out all my feminine accessories and become more butch. I could've had top surgery and identified as nonbinary, or I could have added testosterone to the mix and identified as a man. I chose top surgery and testosterone, not because my new therapist wanted me to, but because that was what enabled me to feel fully aligned with myself. I was not persuaded, coerced or cajoled into transitioning. If, after all our work, I had turned out to be a straight, cisgender woman, my new therapist would have been perfectly happy. But I didn't. I turned out to be a trans man, because that's what I am.

✢ ✢ ✢

Trans people, as I have mentioned before, don't like fences. The only parameters that surround trans people are the ones that were erected by cis people, generated from their limited capacity to understand us, and created with the intention of trying to make us more comprehensible. So cis people ended up defining what we were and weren't allowed to be, which then dictated what we had to perform to gain access to gender-affirming healthcare.

Back in the old days most of the medical gatekeepers didn't understand men and women beyond gender stereotypes and body parts, so trans people would have to pretend to conform to those standards to get treatment. We'd sit in an office and tell the doctor that we'd known from the age of five that we were a boy not a girl, that we preferred blue to pink, and that we felt trapped inside our bodies. Because if we didn't, we'd be denied access to treatment. Even though we no longer have to do this — thank the lord or I'd still have breasts — this image of trans people miserably reducing their identities into a preference for suits over dresses and penises over vaginas prevails.

But if cis people struggle to define gender or sex without resorting to stereotypes or body parts, then obviously it's going to be hard for them to understand how we would explain ourselves to our therapists using any other language. How could they possibly imagine the kind of conversations we have while we're uncovering ourselves? *I feel ... I know ... I'm not ... I am ... this is right ... this is wrong ...* Even we can't always explain what we mean. But we know who we are deep down inside, and when we finally find ourselves talking with someone who speaks the same language, the relief is indescribable.

If you ask a trans person about their experience of being trans you will get a far more nuanced and accurate reply, even from a child, than if you try to extrapolate from appearances, statistics, and data who they are or what they need. There is only one way to find out how a trans person identifies, and that's by asking them.

The extreme position of the hostile cis perspective, of course, is that the people at the gender clinics are "transing" confused cis children, presumably for monetary gain. They can't be helping trans kids, because trans people don't exist. If you genuinely don't believe in trans people, then I won't be able to disabuse you of this notion.

But if you do believe in trans people, I can see how you might still be worried about what happens to a cis person if they accidentally end up on a gender therapist's couch.

In the blog post she published in June 2020, J.K. Rowling admitted that she'd felt ambivalent about her female gender during her youth, and wondered whether, if she'd been born 30 years later, she too might have tried to transition. *The allure of escaping womanhood would have been huge* …, she wrote. *If I'd found community and sympathy online that I couldn't find in my immediate environment, I believe I could have been persuaded to turn myself into the son my father had openly said he'd have preferred.*

It's not uncommon for cis women to question their gender at some point during their adolescence. Maybe they were attracted to other women, or leaned towards masculine presentation, or struggled with a dawning understanding of sexism, or began to realize they were becoming less safe in their bodies than their male friends. If this is what you believe young trans men are experiencing, then of course you are going to advocate for the "watch and wait" approach: Given enough time, eventually the adolescent girl will learn how to accept her sexuality, come to terms with her body, or develop the foundational strength necessary to help her navigate her way through a hostile, male-dominated society.

But these common adolescent struggles with body image, sexuality, femininity, and misogyny have nothing whatsoever to do with being trans. A trans child may have to deal with these issues too, but once they've been resolved, his transness still remains.

A good gender therapist will be able to recognize the difference between a young cis girl who is afraid of having to conform to the gender norms that society is trying to impose upon her, and a young trans man whose dysphoria is rooted in his body. There is a difference between gender nonconformity and gender dysphoria, and the mistake many gender critical feminists make is in conflating the two; they assume that dysphoria is just a side-effect of gender nonconformity, and therefore can be cured by the application of feminism.

Gender nonconformity is a reaction to a social environment; gender dysphoria is a reaction to one's own body. Not a body that feels unsafe, but a body that feels wrong. Feminism isn't a magical drug that can fix a trans body; feminism is an ideology. A good ideology — one we should all embrace — but still.

Transness is not an ideology. I will keep repeating this because it is true.

It is also true that in the past some gender therapists have misdiagnosed gender nonconformity as gender dysphoria and directed a gender nonconforming cis child towards transition. Gender critical feminists pounce on these stories but citing the results of inadequately simplistic models of treatment from the past isn't an argument for ending gender affirming treatment altogether; it's an argument for improving the treatment, both through increased funding and public acceptance of its necessity. But the idea that these clinics are causing harm has become so deeply embedded in people's minds that a large part of the energy that should be diverted into research and education is currently being wasted trying to stop the clinics from being shut down. It's not just individual people but entire organizations that are stuck in crouch position, unable to allocate their resources into improving their services because they're being used up in the fight for basic survival.

There is also a tendency to suggest that kids who present at gender clinics with the co-morbidities of depression, suicidal ideation, and eating disorders are just fucked-up cis kids. Not only is this insulting to people with mental health issues, it also misses the fact that the by-products of untreated gender dysphoria are — naturally — depression, suicidal ideation and eating disorders. When you're trying to change your body without the help of medical intervention, an eating disorder is a likely outcome. Trust me, I've been there.

If we allow kids to talk openly about what they're thinking and feeling without fear of repercussion, an experienced therapist will recognize the ones who have come to the wrong place for support and gently redirect them to the right one. Nobody wants to trans a cis person. What we want is to create more safe places where any person can come to ask questions, find answers, and leave knowing exactly who they are.

It's developmentally appropriate for teenagers to explore all facets of their identity — that is what teenagers do ... And, generationally, gender has become a part of someone's identity that is more socially acceptable to explore.

Dr. Angela Goepferd

What exactly is the danger in asking questions, in exploring, experimenting, showing curiosity? Kids who are raised with love and support know when they are sure or unsure. They know when to step forward, when to pause, when to step back. Children use play to learn, to discover their truth, but it's harder for them to find their truth if it isn't presented as one of the options. If we offer them a wide range of different truths, they'll be able to find theirs. If we only present them with one truth, and it doesn't fit them, we leave them searching blindly in the dark.

Give a child one choice — you are a girl — and they will take it, whether it makes them happy or not. Give them two — you are a gay girl or a straight girl — and they will pick between those two available options. But give them more — gay, straight, queer, trans, bi, nonbinary, pan, fluid — and they'll find the one that fits them best.

Trans kids who are supported by their doctors and families, who are allowed to socially transition in pre-puberty and are then allowed access to puberty blockers during adolescence, overwhelmingly continue to full transition and remain in the gender with which they identify. The data on this is incontrovertible, but instead of seeing it as a story of success, gender critical feminists try to use it as proof that there is something sinister about gender-affirming treatment itself. *It is not so much a treatment for gender dysphoria as a means to ensure that cross-sex identification persists,* Helen Joyce says. But this interpretation of the data exposes the hostile cis perspective, where the only successful treatment of gender dysphoria is one that results in a cis-identifying child.

This runs deeper than an innate bias against trans people. An innate bias holds that transitioning is bad, because being trans is bad; it's based on a value system where trans people hold less value than cis people.

But the hostile cis perspective holds that trans people don't exist in the first place, so the only successful "resolution" of gender dysphoria must be one where all thoughts of transition vanish. The resolution cannot be "being trans and happy" because that would undermine the bedrock of the gender critical ideology, which is that nobody is trans.

Of course, there are always going to be cis kids who see their friends experimenting with gender fluidity and are curious, who will try these identities on for size before deciding they don't fit, just as there were always girls who made out with other girls at parties before deciding they preferred boys. Gender critical feminists call it 'desistance' when a gender nonconforming kid reverts to a cis identity, but since this word is generally associated with ceasing from criminal or antisocial behavior, it only serves to reinforce the notion that they've done something morally wrong. Shaming kids for being curious is not an act of kindness, or, for that matter, of feminism.

Furthermore, a trans kid who reverts to a cis identity because their transition isn't supported obviously hasn't stopped being trans, they've just learned to live with their dysphoria, to the detriment of their mental health. We can call this detransition if we want, but if the symptoms of dysphoria persist, we cannot call it a successful outcome for the child.

We need to believe kids who say they're trans. We need to allow them to ask complicated questions about their own identities, to trust that a child's journey is their own, and support them while they find their way. The well-intentioned of us, cis or trans, are all hoping for the same outcome: Zero medical mistakes, not because people are no longer transitioning, but because each individual child is getting exactly the kind of care that they need.

And if we can create a safer world for trans kids to live in post-transition, that would help too.

✢ ✢ ✢

We passed a law to protect the children ... and I think that's what's important.

Leslie Rutledge

One of the problems with the hostile cis perspective is that it can only be maintained by deliberately resisting any kind of empathetic identification with trans kids.

When people say they want to "protect the children," it's possible that some of them think they're telling the truth, but it's the truth of someone who is only interested in protecting kids who are cis. We can tell them that they are undermining approved medical guidelines for trans kids until we're blue in the face, but it won't make a difference, because they're not talking about trans kids. They are rigidly refusing to factor trans kids into the version of the truth they are telling.

Do they not believe that kids can be trans? Or do they believe in trans kids, but just not care about them?

In my more generous moments, I wonder whether this isn't just a failure of perspective, it's a failure of imagination. I wish these people could step outside of their own version of reality for long enough to consider what this "protection" feels like for a kid who is trans.

Imagine you are a young girl, aged eight or nine. You want to grow into a young woman, and you know that this is possible, but not without medical help. You know that there are doctors out there who can help you become who you are supposed to be: a person who looks like a young woman, who feels like a young woman, and who presents to everyone else as a young woman. This is what you want; it's the future you dream of.

Now imagine someone in authority — your State Attorney General, for example — tells you that you're not allowed access to this medical help until you're over the age of 18. You know that by then it will be too late. You will have grown too tall to pass as a woman, your shoulders will be too broad, your jaw will be too wide, your brow will be too heavy, your voice will be too deep, your hands will be too big. Whatever medical interventions might be available to you after the age of 18 will not undo any of these changes. The future you dreamed of suddenly vanishes.

When your State Attorney General tells you that she just wants you to be able to enjoy your childhood, what are you going to tell her about how that childhood looks to you now? You can't just forget about all this and go play in the park. You're going to spend every second of the next 10 years watching your body change, and it will make you feel sick to your stomach, because this person you are turning into is not you. You will start to feel alienated from your female friends as you become increasingly less feminine-looking, and people will start doubting you when you say you're a girl. You begin to realize that these changes mean you'll always stand out, you'll always be identifiably trans, and as you grow older, you'll learn that this will make it harder to get a job, rent an apartment, have a relationship, or even safely walk down the street.

In the meantime, you know that there are other children in other parts of the country who aren't being forced to go through this, who can just grow up to be young women with the minimum of fuss. How do you live with this knowledge? How do you make it through to 18 knowing that all of this was entirely preventable, but you weren't allowed to prevent it?

When someone says they are trying to "protect the children," let us be very clear that there is only one type of child they are trying to protect.

✜ ✜ ✜

To force young women to compete with male-bodied athletes will bring about the collapse of women's sports.

Abigail Shrier

Are Republicans genuinely afraid of trans people, or are we merely a pawn in their political game? Who knows. Each person's motives are a mystery, often as much to themselves as to anyone else. What we do know is that Republican lawmakers are trying to legislate us out of existence, and they know that if they want these laws to pass, they need to leave no room for complexity or nuance. So, for their propaganda they search for the one area in which they believe the biological difference between men and women's bodies makes an irrefutable difference, and they land on sports.

No matter that the quantity of trans people engaged in professional sports is tiny, it's the premise of the argument that matters. If they can focus the public's attention on a black-and-white debate about body size and strength, maybe they can prevent everyone from thinking about — or empathizing with — the people they are trying to exclude.

So let me try to show you what this feels like from the perspective of one of these people.

Let's call her Emily. While the argument about trans bodies rages in the courtrooms, Emily is outside playing soccer with her friends. Emily's father is the sort of sensible parent who doesn't shout insults at the ref from the sidelines or waste his time dreaming of sports scholarships or professional endorsements; he wants Emily to play soccer because it's fun and it makes her happy. The fresh air and exercise produce endorphins, which help to ease the anxiety caused by her dysphoria; the compulsory nature of the practices forces her out of her bedroom where she's otherwise prone to isolate; the enthusiastic encouragement she gets from her teammates gives her a taste of what real female friendship might feel like. Emily finds it hard to bond with the other girls in her school because her body is not developing the same way that their bodies are developing, and this difference often makes her feel left out. But when she's running around in her soccer kit with her hair tied up in a ponytail and her pink cleats covered in mud, she feels like she belongs.

Emily's dad knows that this feeling of belonging can be the difference between a good day and a bad day for his daughter, and because the world can sometimes be a dark place for a kid like Emily, he wants her to have as few bad days as possible. When Emily scores a goal, Emily's dad tends to get a bit over-excited, jumping up and down and yelling with a bit too much gusto. But that's only because he knows that every small win for Emily will prove to her that she can succeed — not only at soccer, but at everything else too. And when all the odds are stacked against your kid, this is something you really need them to know.

Sometimes Emily's dad thinks that soccer may have saved his daughter's life. He writes to his state's Governor to tell him this, but he's not sure if the Governor ever reads his letters.

The Governor does in fact read his letters, but he takes no notice of them because he's too busy trying to reassert his power over his constituents. He knows that trans people are a threat — inconsistent, unpredictable, and impossible to regulate — and if he can't forcibly expel them from his state, then at least he can make it harder for them to exist. Ideally, he wants to stop it all before it starts, cut it off at the roots, so to speak. He's going to make it illegal for Emily to play soccer on the girls' team, because if she's not allowed to play with the girls then with any luck she might give up and go back to being a boy. And he's closing down the gender clinics and pulling all the queer books from the school libraries and banning everyone from talking to kids about gender; he's trying to reverse the tide back to the days when nobody transitioned because nobody knew that transitioning was a thing you could do.

The Governor might or might not be aware that withholding information is a tactic used by abusers.

At the time of going to press, eighteen states have outlawed gender affirming care for minors. This desire to ban children from transitioning partly stems from the knowledge that people who start their transitions in adulthood are generally easier to spot; if we can't be eradicated, at least we can be seen, monitored and contained. The harder they make it for us to transition before puberty, the less likely we are to grow into passing adults, and if we can't survive childhood without transitioning, then suicide solves the problem. A genocide perpetrated by our own selves, for which they are not responsible.

The short term inhumanity of this is staggering, but in the long term, the governor may be fighting a losing battle. I grew up with zero access to books about gay kids or trans people or queer families; nothing about my childhood allowed for the possibility of being trans, and yet I still ended up transitioning. It may have taken me half my life, but as soon as I realized it was possible, it was a done deal. Nothing could stop it from happening, least of all me.

But innocent children are being recruited, the evangelicals howl.

Are they really? My children have grown up surrounded by queerness, and yet so far, they all appear to be cis and straight. I grew up surrounded by cis heterosexuality, and yet I am queer and trans. The alleged recruiting effort doesn't seem to be going very well in either direction.

Children are not empty vessels waiting to be filled, or hunks of wet clay waiting to be molded into whatever the nearest adult chooses. If that were a thing that happened, I'd still be wearing a dress. I am who I am despite years of everyone around me — myself included — trying to make me into something different.

We fixate on statistics when talking about trans kids, but in reality the numbers are meaningless. Nothing is lost or gained when a child reveals their identity to the world. There will be no greater number of trans people and no fewer number of cis people if we allow people to choose their own path, there will just be people who can be themselves without having to go through years of misery first. People are who they are, and the more information they have, the closer they are likely to get to the truth of themselves, and the closer they are to the truth of themselves, the happier they are likely to be. Kids know this. So do adults, we just pretend not to sometimes.

Maybe one day we'll live in a world where there's room for all of us, where *every* body is permitted and *no* body is punished. Because we're not trying to hurt anyone. We're nobody's enemy. We're only trying to fight the illusion that there's any kind of fence between the people who subscribe to the gender binary — who believe themselves to be cis — and the people who don't. There is no *Them* and *Us*. There's not even a *We* or a *You*. The difference between us is not nearly as concrete as the people who have a vested interest in keeping us apart would have you believe. The only boundaries around gender are the ones we've drawn ourselves, and it's up to each of us to choose whether we want to remain inside those lines. The ability to jump the fence isn't a special talent, it's not exclusive to trans people, it's something anyone can do. There's no reason for anyone to stay stuck inside an identity that doesn't fit them anymore.

When the brutality of the war against trans people overwhelms me, I turn to those of my friends who've spent their lives fighting against injustice. *How can it be this painful?* I ask. *How can people be so cruel?* They roll their eyes knowingly and say, *welcome to discrimination, newbie,* and I laugh and feel embarrassed for my naivete. But then I think of all the trans kids who are out there trying to fend for themselves. They're all newbies too, newbies with barely developed defense systems.

That's when I start praying.

I trust these kids with the keys to our future. I have faith that these kids can set us all free. Against all odds, I do believe in progress, because I must or die trying.

But if we want trans kids to reshape our world, we need to let them live.

Acknowledgements

Thank you to Linc Ross, Tuck Woodstock, Denne Michele Norris, Jamie Cooper and Stephanie Laffin for inadvertently creating the series of events that led to this book being published, to Avery Langston for their review of the manuscript as it found its final form, and to my agent Malaga Baldi and editor Patrick Davis for everything else.

About the Author

The only daughter of an upper-class English family, Oliver Radclyffe tried to follow all the rules: attending boarding school, earning a university degree, marrying a suitable man, giving birth to four children, and moving to the Connecticut suburbs. Then, he realized that he was not a heterosexual woman — nor actually a woman at all. Oliver is part of a new wave of transgender writers unafraid to address the complex nuances of transition, examining how gender identity, sexual orientation, feminist allegiance, social class, and family history overlap. His work has appeared in *The New York Times* and *Electric Literature.*

About the Type and Paper

Designed by Malou Verlomme of the Monotype Studio, Macklin is an elegant, high-contrast typeface. It has been designed purposely for more emotional appeal.

The concept for Macklin began with research on historical material from Britain and Europe dating to the beginning of the 19th century, specifically the work of Vincent Figgins. Verlomme pays respect to Figgins's work with Macklin, but pushes the family to a more contemporary place.

This book is printed on natural Rolland Enviro Book stock. The paper is 100 percent post-consumer sustainable fiber content and is FSC-certified.

Adult Human Male was designed by Eleanor Safe and Joseph Floresca.

Unbound Edition Press champions honest, original voices.
Committed to the power of writers who explore and illuminate
the contemporary human condition, we publish collections of poetry,
short fiction, and essays. Our publisher and editorial team aim
to identify, develop, and defend authors who create thoughtfully
challenging work which may not find a home with mainstream
publishers. We are guided by a mission to respect and elevate
emerging, under-appreciated, and marginalized authors, with
a strong commitment to advancing LGBTQ+ and BIPOC voices.
We are honored to make meaningful contributions to the literary arts
by publishing their work.

unboundedition.com